AUSTIN
THEN & NOW

AUSTIN
THEN & NOW

With
Compliments

oticon
MEDICAL

WILLIAM DYLAN POWELL

THUNDER BAY
P·R·E·S·S
San Diego, California

Thunder Bay Press
An imprint of the Advantage Publishers Group
10350 Barnes Canyon Road, San Diego, CA 92121
www.thunderbaybooks.com

Produced by Salamander Books,
an imprint of the Anova Books Company Ltd,
10 Southcombe Street, London W14 0RA, U.K.

"Then and Now" is a registered trademark of Anova Books Ltd.

Library of Congress Cataloging-in-Publication Data

Powell, William Dylan.
    Austin then & now / William Dylan Powell.
      p. cm.
    Includes index.
    ISBN-13: 978-1-59223-658-9
    ISBN-10: 1-59223-658-8
    1. Austin (Tex.)--Pictorial works. 2. Austin (Tex.)--History--Pictorial works. 3. Austin (Tex.)--Buildings, structures, etc.--Pictorial works. 4. Historic buildings--Texas--Austin--Pictorial works. I. Title. II. Title: Austin then and now.

    F394.A943P68 2006
    976.4'3100222--dc22
                                              2006044651

2 3 4 5 10 09 08 07

Printed in China

ACKNOWLEDGMENTS
Special thanks to the researchers at the Austin History Center; the continued patronage of the AHC ensures that projects like these are possible. Also thanks to my parents, Bill and Jeanette, my wife Stephanie, Kent and Phyllis Wickware for offering up their home, KUT 90.5 FM, the Heritage Society of Austin and the staff of Satay Restaurant for keeping the curry coming.

PICTURE ACKNOWLEDGMENTS
The publisher wishes to thank the following for kindly supplying the photographs that appear in this book:

Then photographs:
Austin History Center, Austin Public Library: 6 (C02263), 8 (PICA 05041), 10 (PICA 17624), 12 (PICA 20213), 14 (C06569), 16 (C05840), 18 (C00049-B), 20 (PICH 00287), 22 (PICH 04111), 24 (PICH 04043), 26 (PICA 14618), 28 (C00123), 30 (PICA 00735), 32 (PICA 03158), 34 (PICA 27166), 36 (PICH 00343), 38 (PICA 28418), 40 (PICH 03238), 42 (PICA 03261), 44 (PICH 05849), 46 (PICH 06235), 48 (PICH 07640), 50 (C00177), 52 (PICA 00959), 54 (PICA 28189), 56 (PICH 00631), 58 (C03842), 60 (PICA 25803), 62 (PICA 06234), 64 (PICA 05218), 66 (PICH 05251), 68 (PICH 06703), 70 (PICA 10082), 72 (C00949), 74 (C02045), 76 (C01281), 78 (PICA 00940), 80 (PICA 25578), 82 (PICA 01930), 84 (C00484), 86 (PICH 04720), 88 (PICA 18261), 90 (PICA 03147), 92 (C00720), 94 (PICA C00507), 96 (C02547), 98 (PICA 16908), 100 (PICH 02180), 102 (PICH 00147), 104 (PICA 02251), 106 (C06760), 108 (PICA 07735), 110 (PICH 06197), 112 (C03734), 114 (PICA C03444), 116 (C01556), 118 (PICA 04382), 120 (PICA 02627), 122 (C03625), 124 (HB), 126 (C03303), 128 (PICA 22199), 130 (C00073), 132 (PICA 01026), 134 (C02159), 136 (PICH 01774), 138 (C01452), 140 (PICA 20594), 142 (PICA 03777).

Now photographs:
All Now images were taken by David Watts (© Anova Image Library)

INTRODUCTION

Native people sought safety and prosperity among the region's springs, hills, herds, and landscape millennia before the Republic of Texas vice president Mirabeau B. Lamar first visited the area and decided that its layout and natural resources would make a perfect seat of government for the Republic.

The first documented inhabitants arrived here in the archaic period, around 10,000 BC. In contemporary times, Native American tribes such as the Tonkawa, Comanches, Sana, and Lipan Apache prospered in the region even as the drama of their hardships unfolded.

The first Anglo settlers set up a small village on the Colorado River, near where the Congress Avenue Bridge is today. They named it Waterloo. When Vice President Lamar was considering sites for the new Texas capital in 1838, he immediately began lobbying for Waterloo as the obvious choice. As Lamar took over the reins of Sam Houston's Republic of Texas presidency, it was finally his call. Lamar appointed Edwin Waller to lead the development of a new town that would serve as the hub of Texas government: a 7,735-acre town site with 640 acres of riverfront property on the Colorado.

The resulting town was a 14-block grid with Congress Avenue running up the middle. For purposes of expediency, Waller erected a modest building at Eighth Street and Congress to serve as a simple capitol. By October of 1839, the city and the new capital of the Republic of Texas were ready for action. Officially incorporated as Austin in December of 1839, the city had less than 1,000 people—but more than its share of ambition.

However, Houston—both the man and the city—was less than impressed by this overnight contender for capital status. Sam Houston never thought Austin was a smart place to put the capital: too close to Mexico, too far from the coast, and too much in the middle of nowhere. Many felt that Houston's industry and geography were better suited to being the center of the Republic, especially Sam Houston himself.

Sam Houston was president twice, once before Lamar and once after. By 1842, Houston was once again president, and when Mexican troops captured San Antonio in March of that year, Houston ordered the archives sent back to the city of Houston for temporary safekeeping. Austinites simply refused, afraid that Houston would once again become the capital of Texas. Houston moved the government anyway. In December of that year, President Houston still needed the archives to conduct government business, so he had them removed from Austin's General Land Office at gunpoint.

The citizens of Austin knew that without the archives, they would have a weaker case for regaining the city's status as capital. In what became known as the Archive War, locals overtook the Houston contingency with firepower of their own before they reached home. Not wanting to shed Texas blood over paperwork, the Houstonians gave up the archives and went home. Annexation into the United States ultimately led Austin to be declared the capital of Texas in 1846, just in time for the War between the States.

Unlike much of the rest of Texas, Austinites were not huge fans of the Confederacy or its aims. But once shots were fired, it contributed to the effort as its duty required. The war never gave the new city a chance to catch its breath, to begin realizing its potential in the marketplace. Like the rest of the Confederacy, necessities were in short supply. Battles culminated in lost men, economic ruin, and eventual Northern occupation.

In the 1870s, Austin was finally given the time and resources it needed to develop. The Houston and Texas Central Railway reached the town, bringing with it industrious immigrants to discover the city's potential, and huge civic improvements like streetcars and public lighting. By the 1880s, it was the State's choice not just for the capital but for the State's flagship university as well. The Congress of the Republic of Texas had put aside the original land for the University of Texas during the city's planning in 1839. In 1881, these plans finally came to fruition.

By the 1920s, Austin had more than 30,000 residents and a reputation for progressive thought. While Houstonians were taking champagne baths with windfall oil wealth, Austinites were making plans to create a hub of culture and education that would outlast the mere waxing and waning of commercial fortunes. As World War II exploded, Austin was in a good position to contribute to the defeat of the Axis powers. It served as a valuable administrative center for the southwestern United States, initiated Del Valle Army Air Base (later to become the now-defunct Bergstrom), and opened a huge magnesium plant on the city's north side to help keep Allied planes and bombs in the air.

When the war wound down, the city found itself with the perfect ingredients for a community of thinkers. Over the next fifty years, the confluence of solid academia, natural beauty, technical imagination, artistic appreciation, and a down-home atmosphere created a culture that is unique in the world.

More than 1.25 million people live in Austin. It's a top technology center, serving as the headquarters for Dell and as a major hub for IBM, Motorola, and Samsung. It's also known as the live music capital of the world, having nurtured artists like Willie Nelson, Stevie Ray Vaughan, and Janis Joplin. In fact, creatives of all disciplines, from poetry to painting, flock here for both the scenery and the scene. The University of Texas at Austin has almost 50,000 students.

Today's Austin is a city of ideas. It is a place that has successfully become many things to many people without losing its character or its charm. And the premium its citizens have always placed on the value of a good idea, a new way to make the world a better place, has not only distinguished Austin's past but also ensures its future.

The 600 block of Brazos Street was one of the original fourteen square blocks laid out by surveyors in the 1830s. The distinctive Driskill Hotel brackets the left side of this photograph, which was taken around 1930. The tall building on the right is the Driskill Hotel Annex, built in 1930 to give the famous hotel extra capacity. To the right of the Driskill is a building that housed business space on the lower section and living quarters upstairs. In the center is the home of a then-recent merger of two popular papers, the *Austin American* and the *Evening Statesman*. In 1919 they merged into one company but continued to deliver two papers to Austinites: the *American* in the morning and the *Statesman* in the evening.

Both the Driskill Hotel and the Driskill Annex remain local architectural favorites. The original building today serves as Austin's premier hotel and is known as the Historic Wing; the annex is called the Traditional Wing. The 610 Brazos Street building received a face-lift and is today a popular mixed-use commercial space housing businesses such as the Texas Book Festival and the Enterprise Foundation. The two Austin newspapers finally became one in 1973, and the paper eventually moved to its current location on South Congress. The property on the corner at 123 East Seventh Street is now a mixed commercial space, home to the design, print, and communications company AlphaGraphics.

When the Driskill Hotel opened in 1886, it was the most spectacular hotel in the state of Texas. Politicians, barons of business, and the city's other great and good gathered for a game of billiards, a drink at the bar, or a haircut at the barbershop. Its restaurant was as exquisite as its steam-heated rooms, and the goings-on of its ballrooms were the talk of the town for miles around.

The cattle baron and real-estate investor Colonel Jesse Lincoln Driskill began building the hotel, shown here around the turn of the twentieth century, at the same time that the current capitol building was under construction. The estimated cost of construction of the hotel was $400,000 at the time.

Despite the manufactured posh of other hotels in Austin, the Driskill is still the toast of the town today. Colonel Driskill fell on hard times and was forced to sell the hotel in 1888; he died of a stroke shortly afterward. But his name—and the Driskill Hotel's reputation for luxury—lived on. The fifteen-story annex, today known as the Traditional Wing, was completed in 1930, as were eight mirrors in the Maximilian Banquet Room that were once owned by the empress of Mexico. Many big moments were lived out at the Driskill, including a meeting of the Daughters of the Republic of Texas, which would decide the fate of the Alamo, and Lyndon B. Johnson's first date with Lady Bird.

Originally known as Pecan Street, Sixth Street was one of the originally plotted streets in Austin's grid design and was used heavily by travelers coming in from the east. Home to a diverse mix of businesses, the street had its share of eateries and saloons from the get-go. Around the 1930s and 1940s, when this picture was taken, Sixth Street's reputation as a place to let off steam had already solidified. The Ritz Theatre, shown on the right at 320 East Sixth, was built in 1929, and was a popular spot to catch a new Western movie in the still-sleepy Hill Country town.

As Austin's entertainment scene gained momentum from the 1960s through the 1980s, Sixth Street became famous nationwide as a seven-block-long party stretching from Interstate 35 to Congress Avenue. Austin is hailed as the "Live Music Capital of the World," and a stroll down Sixth in the evening offers up proof. The Ritz ceased operations as a theater in the 1970s and, going with the Sixth Street zeitgeist, became a venue for live music. Despite the fact that the Clash, the Red Hot Chili Peppers, Willie Nelson, and Stevie Ray Vaughan have all played at the Ritz, it remains a casual, low-key place to catch up-and-coming contemporary musicians.

William Sydney Porter (1862–1910), the short-story writer known as O. Henry, lived in this modest nineteenth-century home at 308 East Fourth Street. Like many writers, Porter had a varied career prior to discovering his literary self. Originally from North Carolina, he joined a wave of Americans coming into Texas on the heels of opportunity. He worked at Austin's General Land Office in the late 1880s, founded a magazine, and for a short time worked at the First National Bank of Austin. His banking career did not go well. He was eventually found guilty of embezzling funds and fled the country for a short time, only to return when his wife was on her deathbed. He began his prison sentence a widower at age thirty-five, and would take up writing short fiction while incarcerated.

When Porter lived in the house, it was a rental unit. In 1929 it was purchased by one of his admirers; the deceased Porter was by then a world-renowned storyteller. Public sentiment was that it should be saved and preserved in memory of the writer; the home changed hands several times between various parties and charities before finally being donated to the City of Austin in 1934. It was moved to Brush Square, where it stands today, filled with Porter's furnishings, memorabilia, manuscripts, and more. In addition to hosting writing workshops and seminars, it's the home of a now-famous fund-raiser called the O. Henry Pun-Off, where the wordplay would lighten even Porter's heavy heart.

Listed on the National Register of Historic Places, the 1897 Phillips Building at 103–105 East Fifth Street was once home to Austin's first Studebaker dealership. The charming Victorian Romanesque Revival building at the corner of Fifth Street and Congress Avenue was originally a grocery store called Heidenheimer, Strasburger & Company, where a loaf of bread would have cost about a nickel. In 1909 the building became home to W. T. Wroe and Sons, which specialized in horse-drawn carriages (the automobile had only recently arrived around the turn of the century). The Benson family bought the building in 1914. They would use the facility as a Studebaker dealership for the next thirty years.

Though they wouldn't use it exclusively for their endeavors, the Benson family retained the 14,000-square-foot Phillips Building for an astonishing eighty years. Throughout the twentieth century, the building's spaces have served as everything from a United Service Organizations clubhouse during World War II to a textbook publisher's factory. The Benson family sold the building to investors Steve Hudson, Al Ranney, and David Wolters in 1998, and it is today a highly sought-after multitenant commercial property. Its location, heritage, distinctive architecture, hardwood floors, and high ceilings have drawn a number of tenants ranging from photographers to software developers.

The Heierman's Building at 121–123 East Fifth Street was completed in 1887 by onetime Austin mayor Joseph Nalle, who served as contractor for the project. It housed a variety of businesses, including a stretch as the popular Hotel Provident in the 1890s, right about when downtown Austin's tree-named streets were replaced with numbers (Fifth Street was called Pine Street when Heierman's was built). The building was primarily known as the business headquarters of the early twentieth-century Austin entrepreneur H. W. Heierman. Interestingly, it was also the scene of the city's first cremation during its time as a funeral home; the deceased was a visitor from Europe.

Downtown has grown up around what was once Heierman Industries. The building is one of the choicest office spaces in downtown Austin, offering approximately 10,500 square feet of Central Business District space for those lucky enough to get in. It's one of the many buildings that has enjoyed the influx of interest that's accompanied a major renaissance in downtown popularity over the last decade. While the once-corporate vogue in Austin was to take to the high-tech hills around the town, the Heierman is in the thick of where everyone who is anyone keeps shop these days. Within a few blocks of practically everything downtown, it's no wonder that there are almost 100,000 people who work within just a mile or two of this building.

As you can see from the lack of pavement, Congress Avenue was one of the first main thoroughfares in Austin, dating back to the town's original plot in 1839. Running directly through the center of the city, the street's earliest businesses generated lots of buzz among area residents. The 500 block houses Congress Avenue's oldest building, the Robinson-Rosner store at 504—shown here bearing signage that reads "A. Robinson Groceries." Completed in 1856, the Robinson-Rosner Building did a brisk trade in the 1860s selling "wine, whiskey and one-horse plows." The limestone facade of the building was renovated in brick in the 1880s.

Today the whole Congress Avenue area is listed on the National Register of Historic Places. The Robinson-Rosner Building served as a dry goods store after 1903. In 1984 the building received a major renovation, including a reversion to its original cast-iron columns. Today it serves as a mixed-use commercial space, housing such prominent area businesses as CIC Finance; the Internet marketing firm Axiomfire; the architectural firm White, Dolce & Barr; and the law office of Seth S. Searcy III. The building on the corner at 502 Congress is now arguably the most beautiful and historic branch of CVS Pharmacy.

The building at 601 Colorado Street was completed in 1881, not long before this picture was taken. It was originally constructed as a post office and federal courthouse, as Austin's need for communication infrastructure increased along with its reputation as a political hub for the state. It took a decade and $200,000 (around $4,000,000 today) to build. The building was the first permanent post office in Austin. Until its completion, the postal service in town merely rented building space in various offices here and there. The building gained statewide fame when its courthouse set the stage for William Sydney Porter's embezzlement trial in the late 1890s.

The building continued its service as a federal courthouse until 1968, though in 1908 its postal facilities would move to another building across the street at 210 West Sixth Street—and then all over town. Today Austinites know the building as the "old, old post office," or by its formal name, O. Henry Hall. Named after its landmark trial, the building was given to the University of Texas by the federal government. The university conducted a massive renovation of the facility in 1971, and today it serves a number of purposes, including a headquarters for the school's executive offices and chancellor.

Jasper Preston, the designer of this building, was one of the first professional architects to move to Austin. The Driskill Hotel was one of his two famous buildings in town, and this Venetian Gothic gem was the other; it was built for the Walter Tips Hardware Company. Tips followed his older brother's lead into the hardware business, but got his start in New Brunfels. When Walter's older brother died, Walter took over his brother's Austin store—which was on this site. He had plenty of hardware available when he hired Preston to design this new building in 1876, on the site where his late brother's business once stood. The interior columns and girders were crafted from recast Confederate artillery shells.

In 1977 and 1978 the Austin Heritage Society bought the Walter Tips Building, as well as the Eilers-Tips Building next door, and exposed the original second-floor facade, which had been modified from the building's original design. The building was sold to a preservationist and is today occupied mostly by Ironstone Bank. The 708–712 Congress address is a prestigious and centrally located commercial space that not only sports some of the most distinctive architecture in town but also enjoys a gravitas-invoking location in the city's financial district—within walking distance from the Texas State Capitol. All of the building's commercial space is currently leased.

The last home to go up in the historic Bremond Block district, this gorgeous Queen Anne mansion at 402 West Seventh Street was built for Eugene Bremond's son, Pierre, as a wedding gift. Pierre married Nina Abadie of St. Louis and the two lived it up during their stay. Famous for his fancy new cars, Pierre Bremond was one of the first Austinites to own an automobile. The home was built by George Fiegel, who built several homes for the Bremond family. Its double gallery and west side tower likely saw a lot of service at many heavy-hitting social affairs. Pierre and Nina never had children.

Today the Pierre Bremond House, like others on the Bremond Block, is exquisitely maintained and preserved. A functional commercial space, the home was bought in 1967 by the Texas Classroom Teachers Association, which had also bought other properties in the area. The building has retained its original architectural style and charm. Its dramatic vaulted ceilings, leaded glass, hardwood flooring, and other period authenticities still make it a gem. Its pleasing topography and lush old oaks have maintained its status as a superb piece of property over the years and have helped the Bremond Block keep its reputation as an exquisite example of upper-class Victorian living.

The Paramount opened in 1915 as the Majestic Theatre. Designed by architect John Eberson, who designed over 1,000 theaters, it's hosted everything from vaudeville acts to silent pictures to Broadway shows. It was the brainchild of Earnest Nalle, and cost $150,000 to build. As its features moved from stage to silent film and eventually talkies, it underwent a renovation in the 1930s—including carpeting and a sound system. It was during this rejuvenation that it took the name Paramount. This picture was taken in 1945. During World War II the Paramount played a significant role in fighting the Axis powers. It sold $8.4 million worth of war bonds and always ran the latest recruiting films; the United States Treasury War Finance Committee recognized the Paramount and its manager for their service to the country.

Following the days of World War II, America's flight to the suburbs and other trends—most notably television and household air-conditioning—took some of the gleam away from the downtown cinema experience. In the early 1970s, the Paramount was scheduled for demolition. However, a few fans saved it from the wrecking ball, booking a number of popular live performances and sparking a twenty-year quest for public and private financial support that would eventually cement the Paramount as a historic landmark. In 1982 the Paramount merged with the State Theatre next door, creating the Austin Theatre Alliance. Today Texans flock to the theater to see both live shows and movies. It even has its own production company. Harry Houdini, Billy Joel, Willie Nelson, the Marx Brothers, and Orson Welles have all made appearances at the Paramount.

The Millet Opera House at 110 East Ninth Street was designed by renowned architect Frederick Ernst Ruffini and was completed in 1878. The venue's developer, Charles F. Millet, had made his money in the lumber business, and in fact had stored equipment for his lumberyard right at the building site. Upon its completion, the theater had an 800-person capacity—making it the second-largest theater in the state (Galveston had the largest). A number of noted performers played at the opera house, including renowned American composer John Philip Sousa. Progressive politician William Jennings Bryan once spoke at the Millet during one of his many cross-country stump campaigns. The Millet hosted a wide variety of entertainment ranging from boxing matches to medicine shows.

In 1896 the building was converted into a skating rink—roller-skating was quite a fad in those years. When the Hancock Opera House opened up, it stole a considerable amount of thunder from Mr. Millet's venture. In 1911 the Knights of Columbus bought the building and gave it a face-lift to assign a Classical Revival look—hence the change in exterior aesthetics. Since then,

the building has belonged to a school, a printer, and, finally, it fell into the hands of the Austin Club in the late 1970s. It remains in use today as the Austin Club, one of Austin's most prestigious and oldest private clubs. This historic building, along with the club's cuisine, appointments, and A-list crowd, make membership in the club one of the most coveted in town.

Built on the same corner as the first Texas State Capitol, the old city hall at the intersection of Eighth Street and Colorado was completed in 1907. The building replaced a previous 1874 city hall building that had been infested by bats and, some say, ghosts as well. While this building was under construction, the city council met in the popular Smith Opera House. When it was built, it looked nothing like what is seen in this 1939 photo. For one thing, it was made of yellow brick. Between 1937 and 1939, the building got a makeover, and this shot shows it immediately after its renovation and grand reopening.

In the 1970s the city bought the Calcasieu Lumber Company's block on Second Street and built a temporary annex for the city council called the Municipal Annex. This was the first step in moving out of the old city hall building. In 2000 the temporary annex was destroyed and a new city hall was completed there in 2004, presaging the end of this building's service as the city council's headquarters. The city used to lease office space all over town, and when the new city hall opened, the City of Austin canceled a number of leases and consolidated many city workers into the old city hall building.

The land that is today the State Cemetery was once owned by early Texas politician Andrew Jackson Hamilton. The cemetery was started in the 1850s with the death of Republic of Texas veteran and leader Edward Burleson. During the Civil War, the cemetery grew exponentially, creating two areas of the grounds: one for prominent Texans and another for the Confederate dead. Around 250 early Texas pioneers and over 2,000 Confederate soldiers are buried here. In 1866 an acre was set aside for fallen Union soldiers, but they were eventually moved elsewhere. Hamilton, the original owner of the grounds, was a Union sympathizer who was awarded the governorship of Texas by Abraham Lincoln upon the fall of the Confederacy. He's buried elsewhere.

Over the years, the State Cemetery has remained the domain of Texas leaders past. These days, only members or former members of state-level executives and family can be buried here. Those falling outside of the restrictions must be not only appointed by the governor but also confirmed by the senate. A number of exquisite statues decorate the grounds, including works by Elisabet Ney, Pompeo Coppini, and Enrico Cerracchio. In 1964 state leaders made an exception to the cemetery's exclusivity by honoring legendary Texas author J. Frank Dobie with a burial space. His wife, Bertha, was buried there in 1974. In the 1990s, Lieutenant Governor Bob Bullock did the state a great service by spearheading a cleanup effort at the grounds, which had gradually fallen into a state of disrepair.

Getting up and down early Congress Avenue could mean using an automobile, a horse-drawn carriage, or the public trolley system, whose rails and electric infrastructure are seen here. The streetcars came online in 1875. This shot shows early Congress Avenue looking north, with the old 1876 Travis County Courthouse rising to the right of the block. Congress was one of Austin's original main thoroughfares as laid out by the city's surveyors, designed to anchor the city's center to the state capitol and allow for easy flow of traffic for the comings and goings of public servants, guests, and visiting dignitaries. Mayor Alexander Wooldridge, who was in office when this picture was taken, was credited with improving the experience of moving about the city, making improvements to streets, public transportation, and sanitation.

Today the capitol still serves as a focal point for Congress Avenue, though the old Travis County Courthouse was razed in the 1960s. The city's trolley system was for a brief time powered by the Austin Dam, and was popular for years, but by the time of World War II the electric railcars were gone and public buses roared up and down the avenue. Today Congress is a popular spot for locals and tourists, with shopping, dining, bars, office space, and a front-row seat for the high-profile celebrations, protests, meetings, celebrity sightings, and other goings-on that the capitol draws.

Not only was the Norwood Tower the tallest commercial office in Austin when it was built in 1929, but it would retain that title for over four decades. This Gothic Revival beauty was just being completed when this picture was taken. It was the first building in town with an electric elevator. It was often referred to as a "castle in the sky," and it certainly was at the time. Only the state capitol and the University of Texas Tower rivaled it in height, and those weren't open to private use. Its namesake and progenitor, Ollie Osborn Norwood, made his money in bonds and securities. He originally intended to construct a six-story building but his bridge partners, who happened to be architects, convinced him otherwise.

Over the years, other buildings would surpass the Norwood in height but its legend looms over any newly built rivals. The 823 Congress building became Austin's tallest building in 1971. The Norwood Tower is still one of the most prestigious commercial addresses in the downtown financial district, and is today owned by members of former president Lyndon B. Johnson's family.

Johnson's daughter and her family live in the penthouse. Lady Bird Johnson once remarked that the building was like "frozen music," though current owner Luci Baines Johnson notes that younger generations of Austinites refer to it as the "Wedding Cake Building."

At 304 East Seventh Street, St. David's is one of the oldest buildings in town—and also one of the most distinctive. The church was constructed in 1853, though the congregation dates back to 1848. This photo, taken around the 1870s, shows the church on what was then Bois d'Arc Street. At the time of its construction, the church was across the street from the home of the president of the Republic of Texas, Mirabeau B. Lamar. The historic Castleman-Bull House can be seen immediately to the right of the church over the horseman's shoulder. At the time this picture was taken, the horseman would have had plenty of room to ride—Austin's population was fewer than 12,000 people.

Today St. David's Church has thousands of community members and stands in the heart of hundreds of thousands of Austinites. It's grown a number of amenities such as a parking garage, a café, and a labyrinth-style meditation garden—but it hasn't lost its historical allure. Some of the church's twenty stained-glass windows date back to the 1870s, its pulpit dates back to 1869, and the church sports an Italian marble altar from 1900. It retains much of its original period dressing and furnishings. A popular tourist attraction for people who find themselves downtown, the church offers self-guided tours all week long and guided tours by appointment. St. David's bought the Castleman-Bull House from the Castlemans in 1963, and in 2001 moved it to Red River Street.

This distinctive Beaux Arts building served as a major Masonic lodge in town upon its construction in 1926. The building's architects were J. B. Davis and W. E. Ketchum. The Lone Star Chapter Number Six, which the building was designed to serve, had been chartered on November 8, 1872, with B. W. Wallace as the high priest and W. E. Floyd as king. The building was made of reinforced concrete and brick, and even had a steam heating system. A number of Texas pioneers have been members of the Freemasons, including the "Father of Texas," Stephen F. Austin. At one point during the Republic of Texas years, approximately 80 percent of the nation's higher offices were occupied by Masons.

Added to the National Register of Historic Places in 2005, the building remains a prominent part of the landscape on East Seventh. It's still owned by the Austin York Rite of Freemasonry; they manage the building and keep an office on the second floor. The first floor, however, is occupied by far more shady types of people: writers. The *Texas Observer* operates out of the old Royal Arch Masonic Lodge, delivering "sharp reporting and commentary from the strangest state in the union." The paper has gained fame and a significant following for picking up stories ignored by the mainstream. A small, handwritten note on the building's first floor reads "Please do not feed the journalists."

Designed by renowned Victorian architect Nicholas Clayton, the current St. Mary's Cathedral stands a block away from the original congregation site of the church, which was first known as St. Patrick's. The building was finished in 1874, operating originally under the diocese of Galveston, as did all Catholic churches in the parish. Austin's population at the time was less than 1,000, so its Gothic architecture was mesmerizing among the central Texas landscape. In the 1890s its striking stained-glass ornamentation was added, along with a restored Barckhoff organ. It wasn't the first church in Austin, however. That prize goes to a long-vanished log cabin, designed by Abner Cook in 1839, that served as a Presbyterian church.

In 1948 Austin formed its own diocese and gained independence from Galveston. Today the cathedral's ornate facade and nineteenth-century architecture stand out next to its glass-and-concrete neighbors, giving a nice overall contrast to Tenth Street. St. Mary's Cathedral is still fully functional, with solid bookings for mass, confessions, baptisms, and weddings. It recently completed a $1.8-million renovation that restored some of the building's structure and aesthetics, including new carpeting, gold leaf, paint, and marble, though the church is planning additional work with an estimated cost of $1 million, for which it is still soliciting donations. The Roman Catholic Diocese of Austin today incorporates 125 parishes that represent nearly a half-million Catholics.

The home at 708 San Antonio was built in 1874, and was originally known as Bellevue Place. The home was built for Mr. Harvey North and his wife, a genteel and well-traveled couple from New Orleans. North was well connected; he even served as an honor guard during Abraham Lincoln's funeral. He was known for his business prowess, but still fell on hard times just a few years after moving into the home and soon passed away. His wife sold the home in 1881 to Augusta Gaines, who in turn sold it to Ira Evans. Evans called in famed local architect Alfred Giles, who added a series of limestone arches, as well as an additional entrance.

The arches, rooftop crenellations, and limestone porch made the North-Evans Château look like a totally different structure. But it's still in the same place, perched in the Bremond Block and commanding a fine view of the Colorado River below. In 1929 the home was purchased by the Austin Woman's Club and has since served as the club's headquarters.

Dozens of organizations use the club's facilities to host their professional education and networking luncheons, presentations, and mixers. The Texas Romanesque building has fared comparatively well given its more than 125 years overlooking the city, an interesting mix of Old Country and Hill Country.

The house at 700 Guadalupe Street was built in 1886–87 for John Bremond Jr., a member of the prominent Bremond family, which made its name as an Austin banking and merchandising power. The home was built by local builder George Fiegel. John Bremond Sr. hailed from Philadelphia and moved to Austin in 1845 to eventually set up a dry goods store on what is today Sixth Street.

Making loans from the back of the store, the Bremonds eventually became financial and wholesaling tycoons in the region. The family owned a total of around a half-dozen homes on the block that came to be known as the Bremond Block, with 700 Guadalupe as its flagship property.

The Texas Classroom Teachers Association (TCTA) purchased the John Bremond Jr. House in 1969 and still uses the building as its headquarters. Founded in 1927, the TCTA and its membership of 50,000 serve as advocates for the interests and concerns of classroom teachers in the state. Before the TCTA, the house had also served as quite possibly the most architecturally interesting YMCA ever. In addition to the John Bremond Jr. House, the association also bought the 1887 Walter Bremond House. After acquiring the property, the TCTA performed an extensive restoration. The home's beautiful Victorian design and the attention to detail given during its restoration have made it one of the most heavily visited historical sites in the city.

The Lundberg Bakery at 1006 Congress was built in 1876. Living out the American dream, Swedish immigrant Charles Lundberg came to the United States in 1872, gaining an apprenticeship at a bakery. Just four years later, he built this beautiful limestone-and-brick bakery of his own, complete with an American eagle. The Lundberg Bakery was popular from the beginning, and over the years gained a loyal patronage from the draftsmen at the General Land Office—including William Sydney Porter. After Lundberg passed away in 1895, the building went from owner to owner but continued its service as a bakery until the 1930s. After 1936 it fell stagnant for some time and was just a subtle architectural shadow in the heart of downtown.

The State of Texas bought the land encompassing 1006 Congress in 1970, planning to put a Highway Department building on it. While removing other buildings on the block, workers discovered stone remains of the 1882–1883 Texas State Capitol and decided to keep the entire block in the spirit of historic preservation. In 1971 what was once the Lundberg Bakery became known as the Old Bakery and Emporium—a center for senior citizens' arts and crafts. Through the sale of handmade goods such as dolls, woodworking, and other handicrafts, plus a sandwich shop, the business lets senior citizens supplement their income while selling authentic Texas crafts and providing tourist information.

The Old Travis County Courthouse, completed in 1876, was designed by prominent New Jersey–born architect Jacob L. Larmour. It cost $100,000 to build, a fortune at the time. At the corner of East Eleventh Street and Congress Avenue, it was at the heart of Austin's growing political scene. Its engaging Second Empire architecture, with mansard roofs, even stood over the official state government for a brief time when the old stone capitol caught fire in 1881. This picture was taken in 1876, as the city was just establishing its links through a railway connection, electric streetcars, and a new bridge across the Colorado River.

The citizenry wasn't the only mass to fall in love with those old mansard roofs. Bats, birds, and bugs moved in and brought their friends, prompting the building's managers to have its characteristic roofing removed entirely. After the reroofing in the 1920s, the building looked entirely different but still fit in well with the architecture of the time. A new courthouse was built and the building became known as the Walton and was used by the state strictly for office space. In the 1960s, as space downtown was becoming scarce, the building was finally razed in the name of development. Today the building site serves as a parking lot for state employees.

Wooldridge Park has its origins in Austin's earliest days. The land on which it is situated was one of four blocks set aside strictly for public use by the city's founders. It remained undeveloped until the early 1900s, when Mayor Alexander P. Wooldridge started an initiative to turn it into a park. Wooldridge was a high-profile leader whose life's work was improving the quality of life for Austin residents; buying Barton Springs was his idea, as was the failed Austin Dam of 1893. The park opened in 1909; Wooldridge could see it from his house. The gazebo was designed by the Page brothers, renowned architects from St. Louis who also designed Austin's famous Littlefield Building.

In its almost century-long history, Wooldridge Park has been a centerpiece of Austin civic life and leisure. Of the four original public squares, one is now a parking lot and, in addition to Wooldridge Square, two others—Republic and Brush squares—continue their service. Generations have enjoyed the park. Politicians such as Lyndon B. Johnson and Huey Long have used its gazebo as a pulpit. Sunday evenings in the summer, one can find picnic blankets spread out so people can enjoy free classical music from the Austin Symphony Orchestra. Everything from human-size chess to sunbathers and poetry readings can be seen on any given day—and the city provides free wireless Internet throughout the park.

The first building constructed to house a permanent public library in Austin was built in 1933 at the corner of Ninth Street and Guadalupe. The 26,000-square-foot Italian Renaissance Revival building, made of Cordova cream limestone, cost $145,000, and replaced a temporary library building that was moved to Angelina Street to become the city's first branch library. Designed by Hugo Kuehne, the building takes up half a city block overlooking Wooldridge Park. Hugely popular with children and adults, the building's craftsmanship showcased local artisans' handiwork, including the wrought-iron work of Fortunat Weigl and the wood carvings of Peter Mansbendel. Darthula Wilcox was the first library director.

In 1979 a new and much larger library was built next door to better facilitate the needs of a city that had grown approximately 530 percent since the 1933 building's construction. There was talk of demolishing the old gem, but the newly formed Austin History Center Association championed its renovation. A combination of grants and bonds, as well as the support of many civic groups, made possible the building's use as a repository for local historical information. The building reopened in 1983 as the Austin History Center after undergoing restoration that brought its aesthetics into line with its original design. The center offers resources on every aspect of Austin and Travis County history, from individual homes and neighborhoods to the life and works of O. Henry.

This magnificent example of Victorian architecture at West Eleventh and Guadalupe was completed in 1887. After making it big in the brick business, Michael Butler wanted more than a home; he wanted a great home. Hiring architect Thomas Harding of Little Rock, Arkansas, to design this Queen Anne–style dream house, he spared no expense. Except perhaps the bricks; those came from his factory, of course. He even trimmed some of the house with granite that was part of a shipment intended for use on the capitol building. It was one of the original Austin trophy homes, its reaching turrets a testament to Victorian entrepreneurialism and the pioneering spirit.

Unfortunately, sometimes the wrecking ball can't be dodged when the market speaks. Yesterday's trophy home became today's fixer-upper, changing hands a few times in the late 1960s before eventually being slated for demolition in 1971. Efforts were made to save it, move it, restore it—anything—but all without result and generally without much outcry from the public, according to preservationists at the time. As Butler's bricks were pulverized and scattered to the winds, several Austinites saved pieces of the demolished house so that its remains live on in homes around town. But all that lives on the site now is a parking lot.

Pease Elementary was founded in 1876; it's the oldest continually operating public school in the state of Texas. It was originally called the Austin Graded School and then the Austin West School. In 1896 an arsonist torched the school, reducing it to embers. The school may have been burned, but the institution refused to die. In 1902 it was rebuilt and Austinites gave it a new name: Pease Elementary School, in honor of Governor Elisha M. Pease, who was a major proponent of public education in Texas. This photo, taken in 1935, shows men taking part in a publicly funded landscaping project, one of many run throughout Texas between 1935 and 1943 to provide a subsistence wage for families hit by unemployment.

A number of additions and upgrades have been made to the building. Today Pease Elementary is a shining example of public schooling for young people. The school has a strong sense of community, and emphasizes interdisciplinary learning that combines math, science, language, arts, and more. Its eclectic, diverse curriculum and student body make it one of the most popular schools in town. What's more, it's the only elementary school in Austin where one can willingly transfer into, no matter where one lives. There are only two classes per grade, enabling the school to maintain a strong sense of community and intellectual focus.

In the 1850s the Texas state legislature decided to build a house that would host the standing governor, in which he or she could live and entertain in style, and which would be "an ornament to the Capitol, and creditable as a public building for our rapidly growing state." The legislature set aside a little over $17,000 for this purpose: $15,000 for the house and the rest for furniture. By 1856 the Greek Revival mansion at 1010 Colorado was in business. The fourth governor of Texas, Elisha Marshall Pease, was standing governor at the time and was the first to move in. Austin building legend Abner Cook designed the home; he'd submitted the lowest bid.

The Governor's Mansion has since been a source of pride, mystery, history, and folklore. During Governor Houston's tenure, he had the bathtub enlarged to suit his battleship frame. During the War between the States, a lovesick gubernatorial relative's suicide on site began the propagation of ghost stories. It's been host to weddings, a radio show presented by "Pappy" O'Daniel, rat hunting with firearms by Governor Dan Moody, and visits by thousands of celebrities and dignitaries. A new kitchen and other additions were installed in 1914. The mansion got its first air-conditioning system in the 1950s, and in the early 1980s Governor William Clemens spearheaded a multimillion-dollar restoration effort that turned it into one of the state's most beautiful mansions. Public tours are held from 10 a.m. to noon every Monday through Thursday.

Construction of the fourth official Texas State Capitol in Austin started in 1881. The land on which it stands was designated by the city's surveyors as Capitol Square, and has always housed each of the capitol buildings. The original capitol was lost to fire, forcing the government into a temporary structure. A nationwide contest was held to determine the design, with Detroit architect Elijah E. Myers submitting the winning design. Ground was broken in 1881, and Myers's creation was finally completed in 1888 with the addition of the Goddess of Liberty statue on the dome's summit. Constructed from native "Sunset Red" granite, the striking structure opened to the public on San Jacinto Day, April 21, 1888.

The capitol continues to define not just Texas law but the Austin skyline as well. It's the cornerstone of Austin's visual identity, and state law actually prohibits building structures that would interfere with certain views of the capitol. With these laws in place, the city's skyline will almost always include the capitol, retaining its stature and charm. As architectural and design fashions changed, minor changes were made to the capitol. After a fire in the early 1980s, the State Preservation Board was created to preserve and restore it. In the 1990s the board prompted extensive restoration and efficiency improvements, including an aesthetic restoration of the building to its original nineteenth-century design and additional underground office space dug into the solid rock under the mansion, which created over 600,000 square feet of new space. The entire facility, including the underground space, is a wireless Internet–enabled hot spot.

Construction began in 1857 on the Old Land Office Building, created to house maps, deeds, and other land-related documentation for the state. University of Berlin graduate Christoph Conrad Stremme, a draftsman at the Land Office, designed the Romanesque Revival building, which was completed in 1858. Czar Nicholas I of Russia had made Stremme a nobleman, but the German revolution of 1848 brought him to Texas for a fresh start.

He left his mark. This picture was shot in 1894, just a few years after William Sydney Porter worked there as a cartographer. In fact, the year this picture was taken, Porter published a short story that was set within the building, entitled "Bexar Scrip No. 2692." It appeared in his own short-lived Austin publication, *The Rolling Stone*.

In 1917 the Land Office relocated and the Texas legislature donated the building to both the Daughters of the Republic of Texas and the Texas Division of the Daughters of the Confederacy, for use as museum space. The two groups shared the building for many years, each making use of a separate floor, until the Daughters of the Confederacy moved its Texas Confederate Museum to Waco in 1989. The state pitched in, after much debate, for a $4-million restoration, which assuaged the effects of age and brought the building to a pristine condition. In 1994 the building became the Capitol Visitors Center. The bottom floor houses a theater that shows an orientation to the capitol complex, as well as a gift shop and information on the capitol's renovation. The upper floors house exhibit space on a variety of site-specific Texana.

The call for competitive designs for the current Texas State Capitol brought English-born architect John Andrewartha to Austin. While his design was not chosen, he would have a bright future in design within the city, as evidenced by the home of German-born Henry Hirshfeld and his wife, Jennie. Completed in 1886, the Victorian beauty at 305 West Ninth cost $20,000.

Hirshfeld made his money as a peddler and shopkeeper. He and his wife moved from the house next door at 307 West Ninth; some say it took Jennie a whole year to move from one house to the other, since she was quite fond of their smaller, more subtle cottage next door.

The Hirshfeld House's carved limestone, large galleries, and red trim are as bright today as they were originally. Eventually, the Hirshfelds founded the Hirshfeld Bank after gaining experience making small, high-interest loans. The Hirshfelds had nine children, one of whom would go on to lead the Austin National Bank. A Hirshfeld continued to live in the house until almost a century later, in 1973. It was recorded as a Texas Historic Landmark in 1962. Beautifully preserved and maintained, today the home is listed in the National Register of Historic Places and remains a prized piece of Bremond Block property.

The building at 801 Red River was constructed in 1850 and has been home to a number of businesses in east downtown Austin. At one point, the property was a Mormon settlement. Some sources say the old stone structure by the creek was a slave quarters. It's been both a general store and a furniture store, though its inconsistent use has not often been kind to the property.

Even in its olden days, the building was used as a flophouse and a place for people to do shady things in the heart of downtown Austin. In the 1970s it became the One Knight, a popular spot for musicians that helped jump-start the careers of such legendary performers as the Fabulous Thunderbirds and Stevie Ray Vaughan.

Today 801 Red River is home to Stubb's Bar-B-Q—a local legend for good food and even better music. Christopher "Stubb" Stubblefield was raised in Lubbock, Texas. He opened a small, seventy-five-seat ramshackle joint called Stubb's, which became the heart of Lubbock's music scene. He wanted to grow the business and after a few false starts he gave his brand to the restaurant, which opened in 1996. Unfortunately, Stubb died in 1995 and would never see the new building. If he could see it now, he would be a happy man—that's assuming he could get in. The line for the 2,000-seat joint is often out the door, the music is loud, the beer is cold, and the barbecue true to its roots.

Brackenridge Hospital dates back to 1884, when it was called the City-County Hospital. The original facility was a two-story structure with a mere forty-person capacity. A new hospital building was completed in 1915, around which the facility gradually grew until the 1970s. The area around the 1400 block of what was then East Avenue saw the hospital steadily expand its facility wing by wing, with new beds and specialty services. It received the name Brackenridge in 1929, in honor of local doctor Robert J. Brackenridge. By the 1940s, the hospital had a capacity of approximately 200 people. In the 1950s, Brackenridge became an accredited teaching hospital.

Today Brackenridge Hospital is the oldest public hospital in Texas. West of the original Brackenridge Hospital, this new $43-million facility was erected piece by piece during the 1970s. It's now part of the Seton Healthcare Network, a group founded by the Daughters of Charity of St. Vincent de Paul, which dates back to seventeenth-century France. The group's mission is "expressing God's love through services to the sick, the poor and the destitute." The facility has a trauma center, an ICU with private rooms, a twenty-four-hour emergency department, and specialty treatment facilities for a variety of practices.

From the corner of Thirteenth and what was then to become known as East Avenue, Austin and its southward expanse around the 1920s and 1930s was a sparse and undeveloped affair. With the exception of the private Bickler Academy and its skyward cupola, seen here on the right, there was only limited evidence that Austin's 50,000 people were making their mark. The thoroughfare of East Street began to see heavy use in the 1930s as the city grew both to the north, with areas like Hyde Park, and to the south, with the city's fledgling developments across the Congress Avenue Bridge. The street was first paved in 1933.

In 1951 East Street was widened as the era of the superhighway began in the Hill Country. By 1959 what was then known as East Avenue would become Interstate 35, providing a high-access route up and down the entire Austin metropolitan area. A dedication was held in 1962 at I-35 near Sixth Street. The Bickler Academy was torn down in 1968, and is now the site of a Marriott hotel; its old cupola is now a gazebo in Zilker Botanical Gardens. Where houses and foliage once bracketed the road, banks and other businesses have grown around the valuable real estate, giving easy access to the capitol and Brackenridge Hospital just to the east.

In 1894 the Austin City Council agreed to build thirty-one lighting towers to keep the Lone Star's capital city shining bright and moving into the 1900s in style. The Moonlight Towers were installed all around the city in 1895, lighting up the streets from a height of 165 feet each. The carbon arc lamps cast a circle of light 3,000 feet in diameter around each tower. Each tower weighed around 2,000 pounds. Electricity was still new to many when the lights were constructed, and not everybody was enthusiastic about the project. Some farmers feared that the extra light would give them problems with their crops. In the 1930s the lighting towers were converted from carbon arcs to mercury vapor and finally to incandescent lamps.

Seventeen of the original Moonlight Towers still survive around town today. In the 1970s their historical value was formally recognized by the state and federal governments. They are now an integral part of Austin's landscape. In the 1960s the tower in Zilker Park became the town's alternative, artificial Christmas tree. In the early 1990s every tower came down and received a total restoration, repainting, and preventive maintenance. They look brand new and completely original save for the historic plaque that each one bears. These systems were common in the 1800s, but Austin is the only place in the United States where so many fine and functional examples can be seen.

Temple Beth Israel was the first Jewish congregation in town. Formed in 1876, the congregation initially comprised about three dozen families. Eventually the temple met in this beautiful Romanesque Revival building at the corner of Mesquite Street (today Eleventh Street) and San Jacinto. The congregation built this synagogue in 1884. It was designed by James Wahrenberger, the first professional architect in Texas to have a college degree in architecture; Wahrenberger's parents sent him to prep school in Pennsylvania, and then to study architecture at the Polytechnic in Karlsruhe, Germany. The congregation's first president was Henry Hirshfeld, who, like Wahrenberger's family, had joined a wave of German immigrants to Texas in the mid-nineteenth century.

While the Congregation Beth Israel and Austin's Jewish community in general would continue to live a long legacy, the old 1884 synagogue would not. In 1957 the beautiful temple was razed and an office building was built in its place. The congregation today worships from a facility on Shoal Creek Boulevard and is the largest Jewish congregation in Austin, with almost 700 member families. No evidence of the grand old synagogue remains at the San Jacinto and Eleventh Street site. Instead, a downtown La Quinta hotel offers up an entirely different type of service, as the 1950s office building across Eleventh Street provides more commercial space.

Palm Park was one of the original four town squares the city's founders set aside for recreational use, the others being Brush Square, Republic Square, and Wooldridge Square. The park was between what was then known as East Avenue, with Third Street bordering the north and Red River Street on the park's west side. Popular for everything from picnics to political speeches,

Palm Park's central location in southeast downtown made it popular from the time it opened in the 1930s, but it was particularly famous for its pool. Its development grew from a movement in the late 1920s to form an official parks department. Entering the 1940s, Austin had around 2,000 acres of municipal parkland.

Today Interstate 35 roars by Palm Park's pool and tennis courts, but the intrusion of urban bustle hasn't taken away all of its charm. It remains a cool green oasis in the middle of all the action, and its pool is often packed with kids and adults looking for ways to beat the heat. People who work nearby stop in for a quick walk or to catch up with a good book, its tennis courts see a steady service, and the pavilion is a handy place to enjoy lunch outdoors. The city has just recently finished a series of renovations at the park, including new water fountains and upgrades for the park's walking trails. The convention center is just a stone's throw away.

JAMES BUFORD TOWER

This six-story Italianate structure was built in 1930 as a "replica high-rise tower" on which the Austin Fire Department could train its personnel. At the time, it stood prominently downtown near the Congress Avenue Bridge and what was then West First Street. Skyscrapers were just gaining traction, with the fifteen-story Norwood Tower easily the city's tallest building at the time, so the Buford Tower's six stories offered a realistic environment for training. The structure cost a little over $6,000 to build and was designed by Rexford Deward Kitchens. While Austin first had an organized fire force as early as the 1850s, it was not until 1916 that the city voted to have a full-time professional fire department.

As the decades passed, Austin's skyscrapers would be built exponentially taller, placing this six-story structure well into the "low-rise" category and a bit of a stretch for true high-rise training for firefighters. Still, the facility held value and continued to serve as a working training facility until the mid-1970s. By then the city had dwarfed the structure and training there was getting hard. In 1978 the city council approved a historical restoration of the tower. With financial support from the Austin Chapter of Women in Construction as well as Kitchens's widow, the tower was both restored and given a carillon called the Kitchens Memorial Chimes. During this restoration, it was renamed in honor of James L. Buford, an Austin Fire Department captain who died in the line of duty in 1972.

When this picture was taken around 1940, the rail tracks from Austin's extensive network of railcar lines had just been moved around so the city could make room for its more modern way of getting to and fro: the bus. This shot shows East First Street looking west from San Marcos Street, a few blocks from East Avenue. Local businesses gave the area a small-town feel even though high-rises were beginning to scrape the sky not far to the west. The residents of the quiet houses in this neighborhood saw Austin grow exponentially; dams would bring to life Lake Austin and Lake Travis, the Del Valle Army Air Base would hit the scene, and World War II galvanization would bring jobs and prosperity to many.

In 1993 the street originally known as First Street was renamed César Chavéz Street after the Mexican American activist who died in that same year. This block now sits not far from its intersection with Interstate 35, one of the busiest interstates in the nation—which many refer to as the NAFTA (North American Free Trade Agreement) corridor because it runs from Mexico to Canada. Despite its proximity to I-35, the homes here—many unchanged since their construction—remain quiet and well maintained. There are still a number of businesses that serve the neighborhood, though some find it difficult to compete with ubiquitous corporations. It's a pleasant place to live, offering easy access to downtown and not as much traffic as one would expect given its location.

This shot was taken from the capitol building in October of 1930. The Great Depression was just hitting, though Austin's largely intellectual industries ensured that the town would fare better than most. The view from the capitol at the time showed the University of Texas and its Old Main Building on the right, along with the fifteen-story Norwood Tower dominating the right-hand skyline. Just to the left of Congress Avenue in the foreground is the old 1876 Travis County Courthouse, a few years after its distinctive mansard roofing was removed. An electric train zooms by in front of the capitol as a phalanx of black automobiles pass up and down Congress.

Today Congress Avenue looks like a hallway cutting between the street's commercial developments, though its lush landscaping ensures that it hasn't become just another concrete jungle. The Norwood Tower strains to be seen among the city's contemporary giant skyscrapers; there always seems to be a new, high-profile project on the horizon. As busy as ever, the head of

Congress Avenue is a great place to people-watch, window-shop, claim a front-row seat for various governmental goings-on, and observe how far Austin has come from its beginnings as a struggling outpost in the mid-nineteenth century.

With construction beginning in 1899, this beautiful home at 1404 West Avenue was built for Daniel H. Caswell, formerly of Nashville, Tennessee. Caswell, like many at the time, prospered in the regional cotton trade. He brokered cotton, acquired a cotton oil manufactory, and built his own gin.

The fruits of his efforts are obvious in this breathtaking example of Victorian and Colonial Revivalist architecture—complete with corner turret. This picture was taken in 1900 as the home was completed. At the time, it was comfortably out of the way in the far northwest part of the city.

Today the house is right in the thick of things. The house was sold to the Austin Junior Forum in the late 1970s, and today serves as the organization's headquarters. The group is a nonprofit women's organization supporting the city and enriching the lives of those in need. In November the group holds a major fund-raiser, Christmas at Caswell, adorning the home with dazzling holiday decorations. It's listed in the National Register of Historic Places and carries a Texas Historical Marker medallion. The Caswell House is showcased and can be rented for weddings, parties, and events, and various civic, philanthropic, and professional groups meet here often.

Charles F. Millet of Millet Opera House fame won a contest for the best prospective design of this building, which originally served as an asylum for the blind. The state legislature approved the asylum in 1856, and the building was built for $12,390 by famed Austin builder Abner Cook. The asylum was closed in 1864 due to hardships caused by the Civil War. In 1866, twenty-six-year-old General George Custer moved into the Italianate building with his wife. Custer had been assigned to assist in Austin's reconstruction efforts, and used the former asylum as a home and base for his staff. Custer is shown sitting with his wife standing to his left.

In the late 1860s the facility was reopened as a home for the blind and was renamed. It remained in service until the city's needs outgrew it and the state appropriated funds for a larger building elsewhere. During World War I, it served as an aeronautical training school, and was eventually assumed by the University of Texas. Known as the Little Campus Dormitory, it was a popular residence and hangout for students, as well as a source of pride on the University of Texas campus. In the mid-1980s the university restored the building as an historical site and today it serves as the office of the school's Urban Issues Program, which promotes urban-related activities at the university.

The first person interred at Oakwood Cemetery at 1601 Navasota was a citizen of the Republic of Texas, not the state of Texas; the year was 1839. The oldest cemetery in Austin, its residents include Lone Star notables such as Elisha Pease, Governor James Stephen Hogg, and Ben Thompson—as well as members of the Driskill and Zilker families. In 1913 the cemetery created this annex at 1601 Comal Street to add extra capacity and offer more accommodation to those with common means. Many unmarked "pauper's graves" could be found on the site. A local monument maker named Anton Stasswender helped design some of the most notable structures and pieces.

Today Oakwood is near what is now called Martin Luther King Boulevard and I-35. Oakwood Cemetery and the Oakwood Cemetery Annex are popular spots for local students, researchers, genealogists, social scientists, and even artists. The Stasswender family is still in the marble and granite business, though Stasswender's Southwest Marble and Granite Works off of Pond Springs Road tends to cater to residential applications that Austinites can enjoy while they are still alive. The Oakwood Cemetery Annex was added to the National Register of Historic Places in 2003. It spreads out over almost 200 acres of land. The Austin History Center offers free research support, including an online database with information about those buried in certain parts of the Oakwood complex.

Before the Republic of Texas joined the United States, this was the home of the French ambassador. France had signed a treaty of amity, navigation, and commerce with Texas with an aim of evaluating it as a reliable source of cotton, charging Jean Pierre Isidore Dubois as the legation's chargé d'affaires in 1839. Dubois arrived at his station, after an obligatory layover in New Orleans, in 1840. As a means of promoting his initiatives, he considered it paramount that he impress the provincial Texans with constant reminders of his homeland's wealth. He quickly established a lavish lifestyle and ordered the construction and provision of a luxurious home that would befit a representative of the French Republic and his sociopolitical obligations.

Dubois's Texas tenure did not go well. Rumors spread of his having passed counterfeit money, as well as failing to settle debts financing his lifestyle. He detested the lack of gentility in pioneer Texas. Matters worsened when pigs owned by an innkeeper named Bullock raided Dubois's stable. Dubois ordered his assistant to shoot any pig on his property. He did, killing a number of Bullock's pigs and earning a subsequent beating by their owner—along with a warning that Dubois would be next should Bullock lose more livestock. This "Pig War" sparked several legal and political battles both at home and abroad. Dubois fled to New Orleans before he could ever move into this beautiful home, today the oldest standing structure in Austin. The Robertson family owned it for almost a century until it finally passed into possession of the Daughters of the Republic of Texas as a museum.

The Treaty Oak is on Baylor Street between Fifth and Sixth streets. Over 500 years old, the tree was worshipped by area native tribes—serving as a place to smoke the peace pipe, perform war dances, and celebrate. The Tonkawa and Comanche people used it as a place of worship. The Tejas tribe thought its acorns possessed magical qualities. It came to be known by Anglo settlers as the Treaty Oak because legend has it that Stephen F. Austin, the "Father of Texas," forged a treaty with some of the region's Native American tribes on this spot. The tall tale is a little short on evidence, but either way the name has taken root. In the 1920s its land was put up for sale. The thought of such a lovely and legendary tree on the chopping block galvanized the public into campaigns of letter writing, poetry publishing, and general proselytizing on the tree's behalf.

In 1929 the Treaty Oak was added to the American Forestry Association's list of historic trees, and was eventually purchased by the City of Austin in 1937. As the decades passed, the tree served as one of the city's prime spots for outdoor events of all kinds, from weddings to merely passing the afternoon with a good book. In 1989 a shameless vandal poisoned the tree with a chemical designed specifically to kill hardwood trees. Industrialist Ross Perot signed a blank check to save the tree. It survived, but only around 25 percent of the tree's branches weathered the attack. The vandal spent nine years in prison for the crime. Acorns from the tree are in high demand, regularly spanning the country to give peace and prosperity to new generations.

Richmond Kelley Smoot, pastor of the First Southern Presbyterian Church, designed this home himself in 1877. This magnificent mansion is made of handmade bricks and has fourteen rooms. Smoot used his study as a home-school seminary. Called the Austin School of Theology, it would train dozens of ministers in the decades following the home's construction. The new estate had four spacious porches, which no doubt gave Dr. Smoot a superlative place in which to contemplate his spiritual lessons. It was known as Flower Hill, a name that it would keep for over a century. Short-story writer William Sydney Porter was reportedly married to Athol Estes in the home's parlor in 1887.

Smoot closed his seminary at 1316 West Sixth Street in 1895, but the Smoot family would have a long legacy on this grand estate. And it was generosity rather than misfortune which would pass the home from its original owners once and for all. Jane Smoot, granddaughter of Richmond Kelley Smoot, donated this lovely estate and everything in it to the Heritage Society of Austin, which moved its offices onto the premises. It's one of Austin's most charming historic homes, and is listed on the National Register of Historic Places. The Heritage Society of Austin gives tours of the home by appointment.

Upon replacement of the Old Main Building in the 1930s, the University of Texas Tower was to be the crowning jewel of the new facilities. They had to do something impressive, as regretful as many were to see the Old Main go. And impressive it was. At twenty-seven stories, the tower is a little taller than the Texas State Capitol. Lights from the tenth floor up were designed to shine orange and white from its earliest days. An article in the *Austin American-Statesman* reported with anticipation: "All the gold leaf work on the carillon tower has been completed and the four huge clocks have been tested and found in working order." The tower was finished in 1937.

Today the tower is a worldwide symbol of the university—and of intellectual and social accomplishment. After a series of openings and closings, the observation deck at the top has now been remodeled and reopened to the public on scheduled tours for a small fee. The facility offers a delicious view of the campus, city, and surrounding Hill Country, and provides access to those with disabilities. The time on the clocks is controlled by an IBM computer. Three times a week, the tower's bells can be heard across campus. The University Co-op has a live "Tower Cam" trained on the building so that Longhorns around the world can get a glimpse when they're away from home.

Built in 1853, this charming Greek Revival mansion at 6 Niles Road was built for James Shaw, a Texas comptroller in the years following annexation of the Republic of Texas into the United States. When Governor Elisha Pease stepped down in 1857, he bought the property—at the time a full-fledged plantation complete with over 300 acres of land. Designed by Abner Cook, who also designed the capitol building, it was constructed of purely local brick. The home is sometimes called Woodlawn, its plantation name dating back to the original Pease residents. The home has twenty-two rooms, more than the original capitol of the Republic of Texas in Austin.

The Pease Mansion remained in the Pease family for 100 years. In 1957 Allan Shivers bought the property as he was ending his service to the state as governor. Shivers added some guest quarters to the home. By the time Shivers took ownership of the house, its surrounding acreage had shrunk from over 300 acres to just over three acres, though it's a very elegant three acres. Shivers willed the home to the University of Texas upon his death, which occurred in 1985. The university sold the property to the State of Texas in 1997. The house is listed on the National Register of Historic Places.

Dating back to 1855, the Neill-Cochran House was designed and built by Abner Cook, who also built the Texas Governor's Mansion and a number of other prominent estates in Austin. It was built for the Hill family—a family that would never actually move into it, either for fear of area natives or because of financial challenges. It was built of native limestone in the Greek Revival architectural style. During the War between the States it was used as a military hospital. In 1876 Scottish attorney Andrew Neill and his wife, Jennie Chapman, purchased the house. Judge Thomas Beauford Cochran bought the house in 1895.

The home at 2310 San Gabriel stayed in the Cochran family until 1958, when it was sold to the National Society of the Colonial Dames in America—a group that promotes historic preservation, patriotic service, and educational projects. The group opened the home as a house museum in 1962, a role that it still plays today as the Neill-Cochran House Museum.

In 1998 the Centennial Garden was added to celebrate the group's first 100 years in Texas. Tours of the museum are available most of the week for a small admission fee, and the facility can be rented for dinners, weddings, receptions, and business meetings.

Dr. William J. Battle, who taught Greek at the University of Texas and would eventually go on to be its president, started the co-op in 1896. Originally located on campus at the Old Main Building, the co-op was based on Harvard's University Co-op in Cambridge, Massachusetts—a place where students could get school supplies and clothing at good prices by collectively taking an ownership in the business. In 1918 the co-op moved into this Guadalupe Street building and threw its doors open to the public. Dr. Battle, who went on to serve the university for over sixty years, was also the man who designed the University of Texas seal and chaired the committee for building the new Main Building and the University of Texas Tower.

Today the bustling bookstore on Guadalupe Street is just the hub of many co-op branches, as the business expanded along with a century's worth of university growth. Its main business today is books; it sells more used textbooks than any other bookstore in the United States and makes more profit than any other college bookstore. A good chunk of that money is invested in the university through philanthropic donations to a number of programs and colleges at the university. The University Co-op has four other buildings: an outlet and its East, Rio Grande, and Riverside locations. The bookstore donates millions of dollars to various university endeavors every year.

Taken from the upper floors of the Gothic Old Main Building of the University of Texas, this shot shows Austin's progress from around 1910 to 1919. The capitol building stands alone as the most prominent feature of the skyline, with only a few lone metal towers daring to loom over the treetops. Mayor Wooldridge had just taken office when this picture was shot, and he inherited a handful. The Texas oil boom that caused Houston's skyline—and net worth—to skyrocket was nowhere to be found in the relatively oil-dry Hill Country. Wooldridge set about improving the town's standard of living so it would be the kind of place people would flock to for both living and working.

Almost a century later, the city's stronghold as a global intellectual engine is apparent by its wealth of commercial development and population growth. By law, the capitol building will always remain a prominent part of the Austin skyline. But as the city grows up around it, the capitol has become more the centerpiece of an economic arrangement than the only thing on the table.

Today almost 70,000 people work in downtown Austin's central business district alone, and an estimated 7,000,000 people visit downtown every year for various trade shows, business affairs, and general tourism. More than 5,000 people call downtown their home.

The Victorian Gothic Old Main Building at the University of Texas was in the middle of the university's forty-acre campus. Construction began in 1882 on what was designated by planners as College Hill. It was finished in phases, with the west wing finished by 1883 just in time to hold the university's first classes. The building wasn't finished in its entirety until 1899. Its first class comprised just over 220 Texans. A multipurpose building, it had thirty classrooms, a huge auditorium, nine lecture halls, and the university's official library. The carillon bells in the building's tower were added in 1929.

In the 1930s grumbling soon began among certain university leaders about the need for more library space. Eventually, the school received a Public Works Administration grant to build a new Main Building, and—much to the horror and sorrow of many an alumnus—university president Harry Yandell Benedict had the Old Main Building destroyed. Ivy from the building was removed and spread around campus, various parts of the building appeared elsewhere on the grounds, but what was done was done. The old carillon bells were held in storage until the 1980s, when they were installed in the new Main Building's tower. They can now be heard all over town.

This compact Spanish Revival building at the end of Angelina Street near Kealing Park and Pool was once headquarters to the Laborers International Union of North America, Local Union 790. The group was dedicated to securing better wages, good benefits, and safe job sites for workers, and started in 1903 with a membership of around 8,000 nationally. This facility was used to conduct local union business such as electing local and national union officials, processing payments and benefits, and conducting negotiations—all during a period when rapid urban growth, road and highway development, and exponential increases in Austin's population were putting reliable labor in high demand.

In 1985 this simple structure was added to the National Register of Historic Places, and today it continues to serve the community, though not just its working population. It's now the Howson Community Center, a multipurpose civic center that provides an accessible space for Austin organizations to dialogue with the community through instruction, assembly, and support. It was home to the first Well Child Clinic for African American children living at the Rosewood Housing Project, called the Angelina Conference. Each week visitors to the facility find lecturers, meetings, and workshops that serve to improve Austin's quality of life. The George Washington Carver Museum is just down Angelina, within walking distance.

Huston-Tillotson College was a convergence of two separate African American schools, Samuel Huston College and Tillotson College. The concept for Samuel Huston College came from the Methodist Episcopal Conference in 1876, and was funded by the Freedmen's Aid Society and a man from Iowa named Samuel Huston. Tillotson was founded in 1877 by the American Missionary Society of Congregational Churches. It was an all-female institution from 1926 to 1935. Both schools offered a number of respected degree programs. In October of 1952, the two universities merged to become Huston-Tillotson College. In this shot, the school's ninety-three-year-old, three-story administration building can be seen off to the right.

The institution is now known as Huston-Tillotson University, having been granted university status in the year 2000 under the leadership of Larry L. Earvin. Many of the university's original structures remain. The old administration building had fallen dormant for a period of over thirty years, and in 2004 the university conducted a major renovation funded in part by the Department of Interior's Appropriations Act. The project included the restoration of the building to its original luster. It remains a small but respected university, with just over 600 students and around sixty faculty members. While it's historically African American, there are no restrictions to enrollment and anyone may attend.

Many of the houses in Austin's tony Pemberton Heights neighborhood were built around the time of the Great Depression, though the Fisher-Gideon House, commonly known as the Pemberton Castle, dates back to the 1800s. Originally built as a water tower, the structure was converted from basically a huge cistern to a livable castle in 1925 by Samuel William Fisher II. It kicked off the Pemberton Heights neighborhood, which Fisher named after an uncle.

The castle served as a sales office for the new neighborhood, though when the Depression really hit in 1932 it became the office of the American National Bank of Austin. Texas architectural heavyweight Samuel Gideon bought the castle and finished the process of turning it into a truly unique and luxurious place to live.

Pemberton Castle changed owners a number of times over the years, and was owned from the late 1960s to the early 1980s by actress and artist Libby Winters Bunch, who found the frame of a Model A embedded in the home's construction, and claimed to have seen the ghost of a young woman who had drowned in the building when it was a cistern. She and her husband installed a castlelike carport in the 1960s. It's since been owned by a state supreme court justice, a Dell executive, and, currently, by Dr. Ron and Linda Barnett, who keep the property in pristine condition. It's one of Austin's most interesting homes from both an architectural and historical standpoint.

Stephen F. Austin was the first Texan to own the land on which this lovely Italianate-style villa off of West Thirty-fifth Street now stands. He intended to put a house there but never got around to it. The home seen here first belonged to Clara Driscoll, a businesswoman and philanthropist often credited for galvanizing the Daughters of the Republic of Texas to save the Alamo—namely by putting up most of the money to buy it. It earned her the nickname "Savior of the Alamo." Driscoll bought the land in 1914 and named it Laguna Gloria after a ranch her family owned in Duval County called La Gloria. She designed the gardens herself and eventually founded a garden club.

Driscoll donated the site to the Texas Fine Arts Association for use as a museum in 1943. In 1961 it became the Laguna Gloria Art Museum and the facility became the original location of the Austin Museum of Art (AMOA). Today the AMOA's main institution is on Congress Avenue, but the lush twelve-acre AMOA–Laguna Gloria still plays a critical role in the local art scene. Overlooking Lake Austin, the site provides an easy way to spend the day between viewing the museum's exhibitions, attending a lecture, or taking in the peaceful beauty of the sculpture gardens. It's a great place for parties, and is also home to the Art School at AMOA–Laguna Gloria.

The Austin State Hospital, originally called the Texas State Lunatic Asylum, was built in 1857 and opened its doors in 1861. The first of its kind west of the Mississippi River, the facility was originally built on 380 acres of land at a cost of $2,500. It was part of a development flood that followed the final ruling on Austin as the state capital, yet upon its construction the area was still quite rural. The grounds of the hospital were renowned for their beauty and landscaping, and people came from all over to walk, ride, and picnic under its tranquil trees and flowing fountains.

By the 1950s the facility had become crowded and Governor Allan Shivers spearheaded reforms to patient management. The neighborhood had been getting crowded, too, as the area around the Austin State Hospital was not the remote enclave it once was. In the late 1960s its leaders split the functions of the facility into several distinct specializations, and today the building serves as the administrative core, providing psychiatric care to thirty-six Texas counties in the Hill Country. While psychiatric care has changed over the last century, today the Austin State Hospital's focus is to stabilize patients with cases of acute psychiatric illness and enable them to reenter into society.

Hyde Park was one of Austin's first electric railcar suburbs, developed by Monroe Shipe in the late 1800s. From the get-go, it was a place where fun came first; horse and bicycle racing were especially popular—as was auto racing, eventually. But people there had to eat, too, and when they did they often stopped into this simple store at the corner of what is today Avenue B and Forty-fourth. Opened in 1906, this humble wood-frame building has become the longest continually operating grocery store in the city. Marshall L. Johnson was the original manager of the store.

Today the big chain stores have the little Avenue B Grocery outstocked and outnumbered. You won't find an in-house bank, huge displays, or rows of computerized registers. But people keep coming for what can be found here: that same down-home nostalgia that started with the Hyde Park of old—and better-tasting deli food than one would expect from a neighborhood grocery store. The Avenue B Grocery offers super sandwiches on a variety of fresh breads and a number of other tasty on-the-run foods, but more importantly the store serves as a kind of touchstone for the community. Hang out there for a while and you get the feeling that many customers don't really need anything—they just want to come in.

During her illustrious career, Prussian-born sculptor Elisabet Ney had been court sculptor to Ludwig II of Bavaria, performed a commission for William I of Prussia, and exhibited her work at the Berlin Exposition of 1856. Returning from a decades-long hiatus from her work, Ney moved to Austin to open this small studio in its Hyde Park neighborhood. Surrounded by the Hill Country, she sculpted a number of early Texas notables such as Sam Houston and Stephen F. Austin. Her castlelike Neoclassical studio became a hot spot for area creatives and intellectuals, and also showcased a number of her life's collected works.

Ney died in 1907 after a life of professional, family, and intellectual accomplishment. Upon her death, her friends preserved her studio and work as a museum. Her associates, those who made the studio a home away from home, went on to form the core of Austin's creative community at the university, state, and national levels. Thousands of art students and tourists visit the studio every year to view her work and learn about her pioneering career in the arts. Two of her life-size statues are showcased in Austin's capitol building. The rich variety of her work, the cast of characters that comprised Ney's world, and its unique architecture make the museum one of the most memorable in the state.

When this picture was taken, the area around Forty-fifth Street and Red River Street was way out in the country, without much to see. The streets were muddy and rutted, worn from the tracks of horses' hooves and solid-rubber car tires alike. As with many Texas cities at the time, despite all of Austin's intellectual and industrial ambitions, one of its biggest assets was its land: there was plenty of it. Austin was more than the home of its residents; it served as a commercial and cultural center, bringing in people from farming and ranching communities for hundreds of miles around.

Today this intersection is right in the thick of things; you'd have to drive a long way indeed to reach grazing horses or barbed wire (outside of a museum). Just west of Highway 290 and north of the Hancock Golf Course, the area is now entirely residential and populated by a number of charming homes built in the 1930s and 1940s. A quiet, well-maintained area, the neighborhood is an attractive combination of eclectic architecture and people. Patti Mora's photo studio, the Red River Church, the Odyssey School, and a number of quaint old homes populate the area near this intersection today.

When Charles Newning of New York came to Austin in 1878, he knew exactly what the place needed: suburbs. And when he learned that a new, reliable stone bridge was on the way, crossing the Colorado at Congress, he knew just where to put a suburb. Along with fellow investors William Stacy and George Warner, he snapped up 200 acres across the river. He named it Fairview Park because the area's topography gave it a "fair view" of the city;

it was Austin's first planned suburban neighborhood. He built two initial developments, and by the 1900s he had the formula down. In 1913 his new posh subdivision called Travis Heights would break ground. The neighborhood was spearheaded by General W. H. Stacy, former Texas National Guard leader; Newning drew up special deed restrictions against multifamily buildings and businesses in order to keep the riffraff out.

By the 1920s, over 150 homes had been sold—nice homes—and suburban living was just now picking up a little steam in the region. In today's Travis Heights, there still isn't much riffraff to be seen. What was once far out of town is now just a stone's throw across the river, offering comfortable living with easy downtown access just up Congress Avenue. Known as the home to a very diverse and sometimes eccentric population, Travis Heights has a progressive, small-town feel. Most of the homes are small, well-kept bungalows. The first Thursday of every month, shops in the area stay open until late at night and a mini street festival takes place, allowing members of the community to get together and stay in touch.

Travis Heights is home to the beautiful Mather-Kirkland House, which was built in 1889. The spacious Queen Anne–style property was once the campus of the Austin Military Academy, which operated for about a decade around the 1920s. This shot gives a great view of the home's lower floors, which were built using granite left over from the construction of the capitol building. The home was built by Myron D. Mather, and subsequently owned by prominent physician Roy DeFoe Kirkland and his wife, renowned author Lena Elithe Hamilton Kirkland.

Travis Heights today is an interesting social cocktail of urban progressive and old-school Texas. As Mike Clark-Madison noted in the *Austin Chronicle*: "South Austin is now, and has always been, both Bubbaland and Yuppieland, both the idyllic countryside and the Downtown Annex, and it's the tension between these poles that makes the place interesting." The home that was once known as the Austin Military Academy entered the National Register of Historic Places in 1978. "The Academy" at 402 Academy Drive remains standing as one of the most interesting structures in South Austin and is a popular tourist destination for people driving through.

This scenic snapshot of the Austin skyline was taken between 1880 and 1888 from the rooftop of the Texas Deaf and Dumb Asylum, which occupied over fifty acres a half-mile south of the Colorado River. The institution was started in 1856 and offered a wonderful vantage point from which to view the city. The familiar dome of the capitol building didn't quite set off the scenery, as construction was still ongoing (it would finish in 1888). The bridge that can be seen crossing the Colorado may not seem like much, but it was the first truly successful attempt to provide access to the south side of the river; previous attempts at building a bridge kept washing away.

Today the Texas Deaf and Dumb Asylum has been renamed the Texas School for the Deaf, and is a well-regarded state agency that's graduated over 10,000 students. It still has a wonderful view of the city, as does the nearby Miller-Crockett House on Academy Drive. Over 100 years later, the city is barely recognizable without the familiar Colorado River as a reference point. The old Congress Avenue Bridge was replaced in 1910, and many of the buildings once seen on the north side of the river have either been swallowed up by surrounding progress or succumbed to the wrecking ball. Many think that Austin's geography and architectural diversity give it one of the most interesting skylines in the Southwest.

Zilker Park in southwest Austin is home to a natural spring that draws from the Edwards Aquifer and other prolific natural water sources in the region's geology. The springs were created as a result of the Balcones Fault. The Spaniards, the first Europeans to explore the area, wrote that wild horses would gather to drink its water, and the Native Americans used to call them the Sacred Springs—believing the water had medicinal qualities. Named after early area resident William Barton, the watering hole was a popular place to picnic and swim, especially in the hot Hill Country summers. The water from the springs is around sixty-eight degrees all year round.

The springs became a part of Zilker Park in 1917 when Andrew Jackson Zilker donated the land. In the 1920s the pool was lengthened to 1,000 feet. The main spring cranks out twenty-seven million gallons of water a day, around which can be found Austinites doing everything from getting suntanned to getting married. The spring is big, with plenty of room in which to swim. The motion of the water and the energy make it feel like a living thing, which in a sense it is. Swim tickets are available for just a few dollars, and the city even sells summer passes at a discount.

The pool at Deep Eddy on the Colorado River was man-made, but its inherent beauty and nearby spring remain completely natural. A large boulder in the river formed the original eddy, and the spot became a popular place for a quick river swim. In 1915, Austinite A. J. Eilers bought the land surrounding the eddy and built a concrete pool to accommodate the steady flow of swimmers. He even had a fifty-foot diving board installed in the deep end of the pool; timely visitors might catch the pool's famous Lorena's Diving Horse act, in which a horse and rider actually dove in off the board.

What was once known as the Bouldin-Roy-Hardin Homestead is still a private residence, now owned by Will Spong and Nancy Whitworth. The two purchased the home in 1993 as the ultimate Austin fixer-upper after seeing a newspaper advertisement for the property. At the time of the purchase, the home had been abandoned for almost a decade and offered plenty of scope as a renovation project. The couple's commitment, creativity, and investment have paid off. The home and its surrounding lush landscaping are an unusual, exotic, and refreshing escape—and the new stewards have thankfully preserved the original look and feel of the property and its homespun charm.

Built in 1854, this beautiful Greek Colonial Revival mansion was originally built on San Antonio Drive for John Milton Swisher. A soldier, politician, and businessman, Swisher distinguished himself first in combat during the Texas Revolution and later in a number of high-profile political and commercial adventures. The home was designed by Abner Cook, and is a good example of some of his Greek-influenced design with the dramatic paired columns and Ionic portico. The home gained considerable notoriety as the home of Austin-born actor Zachary Scott, who starred in almost seventy films and played a major role in developing the horsepower of Austin's influence on the stage and screen.

The home was eventually moved to 2408 Sweetbrush, where the property is sometimes simply known as Sweetbrush—and it is sweet. The reconstruction of the home was handled with mastery, and its stately legacy is a superlative addition to this exclusive neighborhood of around a dozen homes where the median value is well over half a million dollars. In 1998 it was added to the National Register of Historic Places. Zachary Scott passed away from a brain tumor while living at Sweetbrush in 1965, at the age of fifty-one. The mature, well-manicured trees in the area are the perfect complement to the house's architecture.

Mount Bonnell, which overlooks the far west side of Austin, was once known as Antonette's Leap. The old name was a reference to a lady who jumped to her death there during a skirmish with renegade natives. Its 200-foot view of the surrounding area made it the perfect place for outlaws to keep an eye out for would-be pursuers. The Mount Bonnell area began to be settled in the 1870s, and took its current name in honor of Texas revolutionary and Indian Affairs commissioner George Bonnell. By the time this picture was taken around the time of World War I, it had established itself as one of the area's best spots for a picnic or a Sunday drive.

Mount Bonnell is still one of the best spots in town to pack a lunch and enjoy the beauty of the Hill Country. And it's much easier to get to these days; just take Thirty-fifth Street and head west. The City of Austin took ownership of the land, which is officially located in what's known as Covert Park, in 1939. A popular tourist destination, the peak's summit offers an outlook pavilion that provides a terrific view of the surrounding hills and landscape below. Mount Bonnell offers a great vantage point for overlooking the Colorado River and downtown Austin from the right spot. Admission to the scenic overlook is free.

When this shot was taken in 1890, Santa Monica Springs was a hugely popular watering hole. People were flocking to Austin as its reputation grew, and though it offered none of the underground oil riches of eastern Texas and the Gulf Coast, its thousands of natural springs were a treasure all their own. Well ahead of the twentieth-century craze, the locals realized that bottled mineral-rich water from Santa Monica Springs was a hot commodity for its medicinal qualities. This spot was near Commons Ford, a dozen or so miles up the Colorado River from Austin.

In 1890 and 1909, Austin made attempts to construct a dam that would augment the city's power-generation efforts, but both dams failed during a flood. Finally in 1940, the Tom Miller Dam got the formula right, creating the 1,600-acre Lake Austin in the process. As a result, what was once called Santa Monica Springs is today beneath the waters of Lake Austin. The spring's natural water still adds to the area's water supply via the lake, and the lake as a whole generates 17.3 megawatts of power—about enough power for almost 20,000 homes. Who knows what artifacts now rest submerged near the springs, given its long history as a Hill Country oasis?

INDEX